ANIMALS OF MASS DESTRUCTION

GOPHERS

Gareth Stevens
PUBLISHING

By Julia McDonnell

Please visit our website, www.garethstevens.com. For a free color catalog of all our high-quality books, call toll free 1-800-542-2595 or fax 1-877-542-2596.

Library of Congress Cataloging-in-Publication Data

McDonnell, Julia.
Gophers / by Julia McDonnell.
   p. cm. — (Animals of mass destruction)
Includes index.
ISBN 978-1-4824-1047-1 (pbk.)
ISBN 978-1-4824-1048-8 (6-pack)
ISBN 978-1-4824-1046-4 (library binding)
1. Pocket gophers —Juvenile literature. I.McDonnell, Julia, 1979-. II. Title.
QL737.R654 M38 2015
599.35—d23

First Edition

Published in 2015 by
Gareth Stevens Publishing
111 East 14th Street, Suite 349
New York, NY 10003

Copyright © 2015 Gareth Stevens Publishing

Designer: Andrea Davison-Bartolotta
Editor: Therese Shea

Photo credits: Cover, pp. 1 (main), 18 Helen H. Richardson/The Denver Post via Getty Images; cover, p. 1 (inset) © iStockphoto.com/susafri; series art (all textured backgrounds, yellow striped line) Elisanth/Shutterstock.com; series art (caption boxes) Fatseyeva/Shutterstock.com; series art (blue boxes) Tracie Andrews/Shutterstock.com; p. 4 © iStockphoto.com/mguntow; pp. 4–5 Gillian Bowser/NPS/Wikimedia Commons; pp. 6–7 (main) Foxtrot101/iStock/Thinkstock; p. 7 (gopher) Joe McDonald/Visuals Unlimited/Getty Images; p. 7 (prairie dog) Lyle Mallen/iStock/Thinkstock; pp. 8, 14, 16, 16–17, 18–19 Tom McHugh/Photo Researchers/Getty Images; pp. 8–9 Richard R. Hansen/Photo Researchers/Getty Images; pp. 10–11, 28–29 Jeff Foott/Discovery Channel Images/Getty Images; pp. 12–13 © iStockphoto.com/beamond_creative; pp. 14–15 © iStockphoto.com/pstraziuso; p. 20 Mare Salerno/Shutterstock.com; pp. 20–21 © iStockphoto.com/emmgunn; p. 22 © iStockphoto.com/tupungato; pp. 22–23 © iStockphoto.com/kyokosuzuki; p. 23 (inset) Kyslynskyy/iStock/Thinkstock; p. 24 Samuel R. Maglione/Photo Researchers/Getty Images; pp. 24–25 Richard Fitzer/Shutterstock.com; pp. 26–27 Dominic Sherony/Wikimedia Commons.

Printed in the United States of America

CPSIA compliance information: Batch #CS15GS: For further information contact Gareth Stevens, New York, New York at 1-800-542-2595.

CONTENTS

Words in the glossary appear in **bold** type the first time they are used in the text.

FRIEND OR FOE?

If you look out over a yard, park, or field and see small mounds of dirt piled everywhere, there's a good chance you're in gopher country. Gophers are little and furry. They nibble on plants with their ratlike teeth, pop their heads out of holes in the ground, and scurry about. Cute, right? Don't be fooled!

Gophers can cause major **destruction**. Read more to learn about the problems they create as well as some surprising ways they help the **environment**.

Chew On This!

Gophers remove dirt from **burrows** by using their head and front feet to push it to the surface—just like a bulldozer!

4

Gopher fur is usually a shade of brown, but some gophers are almost black and others are nearly white.

5

THE RODENT FAMILY

Gophers are rodents. Besides gophers, the rodent group includes groundhogs, prairie dogs, gerbils, guinea pigs, rats, mice, and squirrels. All animals in this group have two pairs of incisors, which are long sharp teeth, at the front of their mouth. The teeth grind against each other, which keeps them sharp. These teeth keep growing throughout a rodent's life!

Since groundhogs, prairie dogs, and gophers all live in burrows, they're sometimes mistaken for each other. However, there are differences if you look closely.

	gopher	prairie dog	groundhog
length	5 to 14 inches (13 to 36 cm)	about 12 inches (30 cm)	up to 20 inches (51 cm)
weight	up to 2 pounds (0.9 kg)	up to 3.5 pounds (1.6 kg)	up to 13 pounds (5.9 kg)
tail	mostly bare	furry	bushy

gopher

prairie dog

groundhog

When pictured side by side, you can see the differences between these three kinds of rodents.

7

WHAT THEY LOOK LIKE

Sometimes people call other animals gophers, such as moles and ground squirrels. However, the true gopher is the pocket gopher. Pocket gophers have fur-lined pouches in their cheeks for carrying food. They're about 5 to 14 inches (13 to 36 cm) long and weigh up to 2 pounds (0.9 kg).

Gophers are built for life underground. Their strong front legs, long teeth, and sharp claws are perfect digging tools. They can fit into tight spaces, and their whiskers help them **navigate** in the dark.

gopher tail

Chew On This!

Rodents don't sweat when they're hot. A gopher's bare tail helps it cool down by letting body heat escape.

This gopher has packed its cheek pouches full of food.

GOPHERS ON THE MAP

There are more than 30 kinds, or species, of pocket gophers throughout North and Central America. Their territory stretches from southern Canada to Panama. While some gophers live in Florida, most call the central and western parts of the United States home.

Gophers are found in many kinds of **habitats**, including meadows, grasslands, and even deserts. They look for soft soil where they can tunnel easily. Gophers usually avoid wooded areas where large tree roots would get in their way.

Chew On This!

It's thought that a gopher can move more than 1 ton (0.9 mt) of soil in a year. That's a lot of digging!

A gopher's nose is a special shape to keep dirt from getting into it.

11

TUNNELS AND BURROWS

A gopher's burrow gives it shelter from the weather and protection from predators. Gophers dig burrows just below the surface so they can easily feed on roots from above. The burrows may include separate rooms for storing food, raising babies, and getting rid of body waste. Burrows can be as deep as 6 feet (1.8 m) and may contain 800 feet (244 m) of tunnels!

Some gophers live their entire lives in the same burrow. Others create new homes in search of **mates** or food.

Chew On This!

Unlike their groundhog relatives, gophers don't **hibernate**. They're active all winter long and live off stored food.

A gopher's burrow may have many "pop holes" filled with loose dirt. The gopher can pop its head up and look around for food.

PASS THE PLANTS, PLEASE

Gophers are **herbivores**. Underground, they eat roots. Aboveground, they eat a variety of plants (usually whatever they can find close to a burrow's entrance). They also may nibble on tree bark.

Gophers often feed at night, quickly stuffing their cheek pouches. Once they're back in their burrow, they may eat the food right away or store it for later. They can enjoy the food underground and not have to keep a watchful eye for their dangerous predators.

14

Gophers get the water their bodies need from the plants they eat.

GOING IT ALONE

Even though they have plenty of room for guests in their underground homes, gophers like to live on their own. Gophers are only willing to share a burrow with a mate or their babies.

In fact, they usually get upset if another gopher finds its way into their burrow. They try to scare it off by clicking their teeth. Other sounds gophers make include shrieks when they're scared and crying sounds when they're in pain!

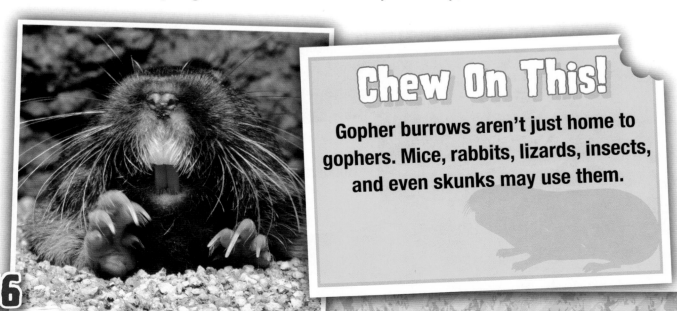

Chew On This!

Gopher burrows aren't just home to gophers. Mice, rabbits, lizards, insects, and even skunks may use them.

This gopher is hoping its teeth, claws, and noises will keep other animals away!

17

GOPHER AFTER GOPHER

Gopher problems can multiply quickly because gophers can have many babies in a short amount of time. Female gophers usually have three or four babies at a time. Gophers that live in colder places give birth once a year. However, those that live in warmer areas can have several babies several times each year.

A gopher baby leaves its mother's burrow about 2 months after it's born. It's able to live on its own, find its own food, and dig a burrow.

Big gopher families mean more burrows and holes in an area.

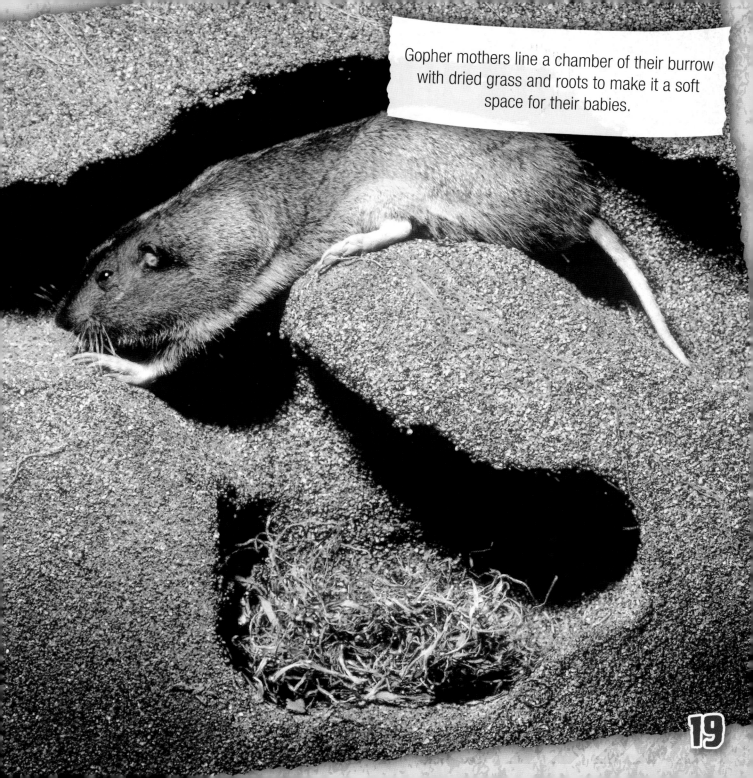

Gopher mothers line a chamber of their burrow with dried grass and roots to make it a soft space for their babies.

WATCH OUT!

Even though they're small, gophers can cause big problems for plants and animals. Trees are weakened when their roots are chewed. Sometimes their roots are uncovered by burrowing gophers. Trees with **damaged** roots may fall over and die.

Soil that gophers push out of their burrows can crush plants. Cows, horses, and people can step into gopher holes and hurt themselves. The presence of gophers encourages their natural predators to stay nearby, which can mean trouble for other animals.

gopher hole

This gopher pop hole blends into its surroundings. It's easy to see how a larger animal wouldn't notice it.

A PEST TO PEOPLE

Gophers and people definitely don't mix! Farmers and ranchers complain that gophers eat their crops and damage fields. This can cost them a lot of money. In neighborhoods, gophers ruin vegetable and flower gardens. They dig up yards and even chew through hoses, cables, and pipes.

Gophers make holes in sports fields, golf courses, and playgrounds. Gopher burrows can weaken dams made out of soil. Also, gophers draw animals that eat them, such as **badgers**, to the area. Many people think badgers are pests, too.

CAUTION WATCH FOR GOPHER HOLES

Gophers aren't trying to be pests. They're just trying to find something to eat!

badger

23

PREDATORS

A gopher's sharp teeth and claws aren't enough to keep it safe against larger, hungry predators. There are many animals that consider gophers a tasty meal. Foxes and cats chase gophers when they come out of their burrows. Birds of prey, such as hawks and owls, hunt them from the air.

Snakes, badgers, and weasels may even try to hunt a gopher in its home. But if the gopher senses danger in time, it will create a wall of dirt to block the way.

A bird with a long neck has the ability to get farther into a gopher's burrow.

Chew On This!

Gophers can run backward almost as fast as they can run forward, a useful skill when they're being chased in a burrow. Their tail helps them feel the way.

GO AWAY, GOPHER!

Once gophers settle somewhere, it's hard to get them to go away. That's why some people bring in gopher predators to do the job. However, some, like snakes, don't eat much, and others, like owls, may or may not be successful.

If people flood fields to drown or drive out gophers, the animals come back once the water is gone. If poisonous gas is pumped into tunnels, gophers make a wall of dirt to block it. Many people end up using traps and other kinds of poison.

Chew On This!

Using poison to kill gophers can be dangerous to other animals and even pets. That's why many people use gopher traps.

Gophers are sometimes called "salamanders." That might come from their nickname "sandy mounders," which they earned because of the dirt piles they create.

NOT ALL BAD

It's important to know that gophers help the environment, too. Their digging mixes the soil, which makes it healthier for plants. When dirt is moved to new locations, seeds are spread so plants can grow. Gopher waste is also a good **fertilizer**.

Other animals, such as lizards and toads, use old tunnels for shelters. Gophers are also an important part of their habitat's food chain. So, if a gopher moves into your neighborhood, remember that it can bring some good along with the destruction!

Chew On This!

When Washington **volcano** Mount St. Helens **erupted** in 1980, gophers stayed underground and were unharmed. Their digging mixed the fallen ash with fresh soil and helped plants grow again.

Gophers in the wild do a lot to help their habitats. Hopefully, in the future, we can live peacefully with these rodents.

29

GLOSSARY

badger: a digging animal related to the weasel that has short legs, strong claws, and a thick coat

burrow: a hole made by an animal in which it lives or hides

damage: harm. Also, to cause harm.

destruction: the state of being destroyed or ruined

environment: the natural world in which a plant or animal lives

erupt: burst forth

fertilizer: something that makes soil better for growing crops and other plants

habitat: the natural place where an animal or plant lives

herbivore: an animal that feeds only or mainly on plants

hibernate: to be in a sleeplike state for an extended period of time, usually during winter

mate: one of two animals that come together to produce babies

navigate: to find and follow a path from one place to another

volcano: an opening in a planet's surface through which hot, liquid rock sometimes flows

FOR MORE INFORMATION

Books

Jennings, Terry Catasús. *Gopher to the Rescue! A Volcano Recovery Story.* Mount Pleasant, SC: Sylvan Dell Publishing, 2012.

Zobel, Derek. *Gophers.* Minneapolis, MN: Bellwether Media, 2012.

Websites

Animals—PawNation
animals.pawnation.com
Search for gophers and many other animals, and find links to articles about them.

Pocket Gophers
animaldiversity.ummz.umich.edu/site/accounts/information/Geomyidae.html
Learn lots more about the lives of pocket gophers.

Pocket Gophers
www.extension.org/pages/9033/pocket-gophers
Read more pocket gopher facts.

INDEX